Editing: Jan Burgess

Design: Peter Luff
Keith Faulkner

Picture research: Michelle Masek

Photo credits: Heather Angel;
Aquila Photographics; A–Z
Botanical Collection; Roy
Lancaster; Natural History
Photographic Agency;
Picturepoint; John Whitehead

First published in Great Britain in 1982 by
Macmillan Children's Books under the series title
Macmillan Countryside Books

This edition published in 1987 by
Treasure Press
59 Grosvenor Street
London W1

© Macmillan Publishers Limited 1982

ISBN 1 85051 178 0

Printed in Austria

Endpapers
1. Alder
2. Beech
3. Yew
4. Willow
5. Elm
6. Birch
7. Horse chestnut
8. Ash
9. Oak

TREES

ROY LANCASTER

TREASURE PRESS

Contents

How a Tree Works

You can think of a tree as an amazing machine made up of many parts. Each part has its own special job to do. At the bottom there are the roots. These may be long and powerful, or short and delicate. The long roots anchor the tree in the ground and stop it from blowing over. The delicate roots search out and absorb food and water from the upper layers of the soil. Next, there is the rigid trunk which rises above the ground to support the branches. The main branches divide into smaller ones to form a spreading crown. On the smallest branches, the leaves, flowers and fruit are carried.

Just as important are the parts hidden beneath the bark. Here are found the channels which carry the sap from the roots to the leaves and back again. These channels are smaller than the eye can see. They are delicate and need the protection of the bark. When a tree is old enough, it flowers and produces fruit. Within the fruit, there is the germ of a new tree.

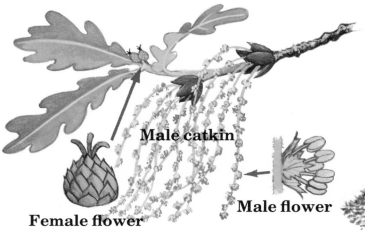

Male catkin

Male flower

Female flower

The flowers of a tree are the means by which the tree bears fruit which will grow into new trees. The flower usually has both male and female parts. Sometimes the male and female flowers are on separate trees. Pollen from the male part must reach the ovules of the female for fruit to be formed. In the case of the oak, pollen from the male is blown by the wind.

Trunk

Leaves

Blade

Oak leaf

Stem

The leaves are the centres of power in the tree. Although they seem thin and delicate, they are quite tough. They use the power of the sun to turn raw foodstuffs into energy for growth. Leaves are arranged on the branches in such a way that each may catch as much light as possible.

Stalk

Seed

Acorn

Branches

The fruit of a tree only develops once the female flower has been pollinated. The fruit then swells and the seed or seeds inside it begin to ripen. Once the seeds are ripe, the fruit falls to the ground. Fruits come in many shapes and sizes. Acorns are the fruit of the oak. They are fleshy and, when ripe, are protected by a tough, hard shell.

Roots

Feeding roots

A Tree for All Seasons

The beech is one of the most distinct and lovely of all trees in Britain and Europe. It grows very tall and has a large crown of branches. It is deciduous, so it has four different faces, one each for winter, spring, summer and autumn. In winter, the grey trunk rises like a mighty pillar above dead brown leaves. Spring brings warmth to make the sap rise. Then the buds burst open as the young leaves grow. The crown turns a delicate pale green. In summer, there are many leaves. The heavy crown creates a dense shade where few other plants will grow. Autumn brings different conditions. The leaves change colour before falling to the ground.

The flowers appear with the young leaves in spring. The beech has separate male and female flowers. The male flowers grow in small round heads on drooping stalks. The female flowers grow in pairs. Once pollinated, the female flowers develop into small, brown, three-cornered nuts.

In spring, when the soil begins to warm up, the awakening roots absorb water. Gradually, the slender, spindle-shaped buds begin to swell with sap.

The protective bud scales expand and then fall away as the new shoot emerges. The new shoot grows longer each day. As it grows, pale-green, silky leaves gradually unfold. Each new leaf turns to catch the light. You can see them shining in sunlight. Another year, another cycle of life, begins.

In autumn, the colder nights and shorter days cause the leaves to change from green to yellow and gold. Then they break away from the branches. They fall with the fruits to form richly coloured carpets at the base of the tree.

In winter, the beech tree stands bare of its leaves, which lie dead and brown on the ground. Now its silvery-grey bark and slender shoots can be clearly seen. If you can, stand beneath a beech, and look up at the delicate pattern above.

The Bark and Trunks of Trees

There are two kinds of bark, the outer and inner. The outer bark is made of tough corky wood which died long ago. It is often very thick and stringy, or spongy. The outer bark helps protect the tree from injury from heat and cold, from animals and even from vandalism. More important, however, is the inner bark which lies beneath. It contains many tubes or channels. These carry food from the leaves to all parts of the tree, but especially to the growing parts such as the roots and shoots.

Beneath the inner bark is the sapwood. This contains tubes or channels which carry water and raw foodstuffs from the roots up to the leaves. The sapwood is also used by the tree to store food. Between these two layers lies a thin film-like layer called the cambium. From the cambium, new sapwood and new bark grow.

The cambium is so delicate that it is protected by the bark. If the bark is damaged, the wound may be infected by disease and the tree may die. If the bark is removed from right around the trunk, the tree will also die. The centre of the trunk is known as the heartwood. It is made of dead wood which is specially strengthened so that it allows the trunk to bend and move in the wind without breaking.

Barks vary in texture and colour as well as in thickness. Trees with thin bark are more easily damaged. In the wild they are most often found growing close together in forests. Here, their bark is protected from hot sun or freezing cold. Some trees have a colourful or ornamental bark. These are favourites for planting in gardens and parks where they can be seen and admired by the public. The barks of some trees contain important chemicals such as tannin. This is used to cure leather. It prevents animal skins from rotting and keeps them supple.

The London plane has a thin brown or grey bark. It falls away in large flakes as it gets old. The new bark is pale yellow, cream o grey-green. The old and the new bark together create a colourful patchwork effect. It is specially pleasing to see in winter when th sun is shining, and it gives the tr a mottled look.

When it gets old, the sweet chestnut has a dark greyish-brown, ridged bark. The ridges often form spirals around the trunk. Sometimes, sucker shoots appear in dense clusters. They make knobbly, wart-like outgrowths called burrs to develop on the trunk. When it rains hard, the water runs down the grooves in the bark like tiny rivers, seeping into the ground at the base of the trunk. Young trees grow very strongly and fast. Their bark is quite different. It is thinner, smoother and pale grey in colour. Gradually, as the young tree grows older the bark becomes thicker and rougher. It also gets darker in colour.

The yew has a thin bark, which i pale or greyish-brown. It flakes away in strips or patches to shov the reddish new bark underneat Young trees have dark flaky bark. It rarely sees the light of day because of the dense, leafy branches. As in the sweet chestnut, old yew trees sometime develop burrs on their trunks. This helps give them rather a quaint appearance. You can also sometimes see the bark on old exposed roots. See if you can spo any next time you find a yew tree

The birch is one of the most easily recognized of all trees, due to its silvery-white bark. This is very thin and becomes papery and loose as it ages. It peels away, often in large sheets, to reveal the new bark. Its bright colour reflects the light. On old trees, the bark becomes darker and rougher, especially at the base of the trunk.

The Austrian pine has strong thick bark. On older trees, this forms long, uneven ridges which run down the stout trunk. In colour, the Austrian pine is dark grey and blackish-brown. It has none of the reddish-orange colour of the Scots pine. This helps to make it look a much more rugged tree. It is easily recognizable.

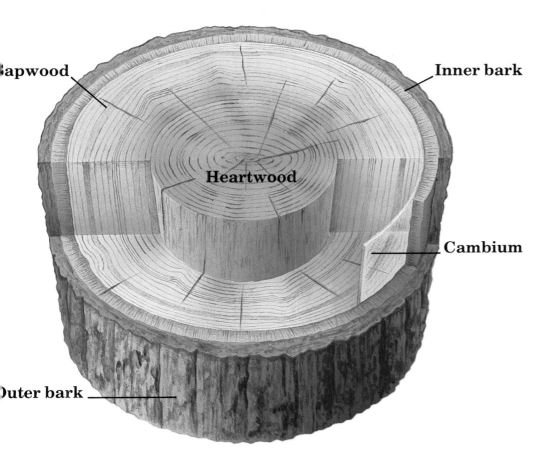

Sapwood

Inner bark

Heartwood

Cambium

Outer bark

The cross-section of a tree-trunk shows two layers of bark covering the trunk. The older, outer bark grows from the younger, inner bark. New bark arises from a thin sleeve of cells known as the cambium. This very important and delicate part of the tree is protected by the outer bark. Without this outer bark, the cambium would dry out and die, and so would the tree. As the trunk grows outwards, the bark expands. This often causes the old bark to crack or flake away. This can result in tree disease.

Each type of tree has its own pattern of bark. Bark rubbing is a way of reproducing the pattern. Place a piece of plain paper on the bark, then rub a soft crayon carefully over the paper. Slowly the pattern will emerge. Try rubbing several different trees like this to compare the bark patterns. Bark rubbings can look very different from one another. Barks with grooves and ridges will produce a strong bold pattern. Use crayons of different colours to create more interesting effects.

The Leaves

Leaves come in many shapes and sizes depending on the kind of tree. Each tree has its own basic shape. All ash trees, for example, have a central stalk with several leaflets on either side. Pines have needle-like leaves, usually in pairs or in bundles. The leaves of some trees are very large, like those of a palm. Other trees have small leaves, like those of the box. Leaves also vary in other ways. Some have teeth along their margins. Some are hairy, others are smooth. There are dull leaves and shiny ones. Some are soft and fragile, others are hard, leathery and even prickly like the holly.

Some leaves are deciduous, falling each year in autumn. Others are evergreen and stay on the tree for two years or more. The leaves are arranged to catch all the available light. It has been estimated that a large oak tree carries as many as 250,000 leaves in summer. Each leaf is working like a little green factory, making food for the tree.

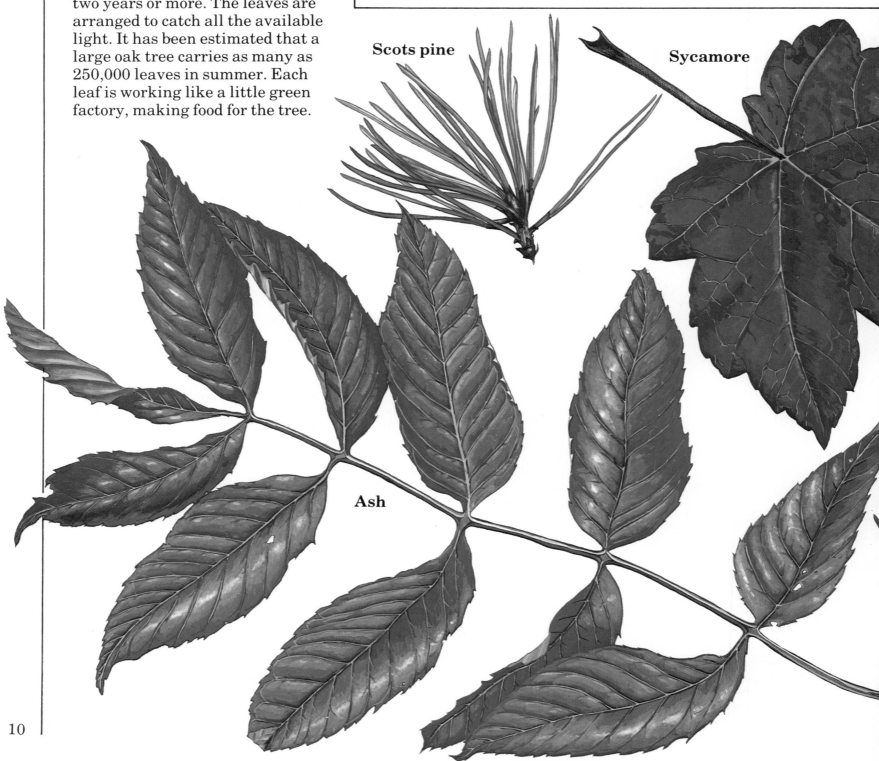

Green chlorophyll in cells
Channels carrying sap from roots
Upper layer of leaf
Main vein
Blade
Stalk
Minor vein
Lower layer of leaf
Breathing pore
Channels sending food and energy to other parts of the tree

The leaf is the centre of power in the tree. Inside the leaf, sap from the roots and gases from the air are mixed. They are changed by the power of the sun into energy for growth. The green colour of leaves comes from special cells which contain chlorophyll. These cells are very important to the tree and help it release energy. Without chlorophyll, the tree would die.

Scots pine

Sycamore

Ash

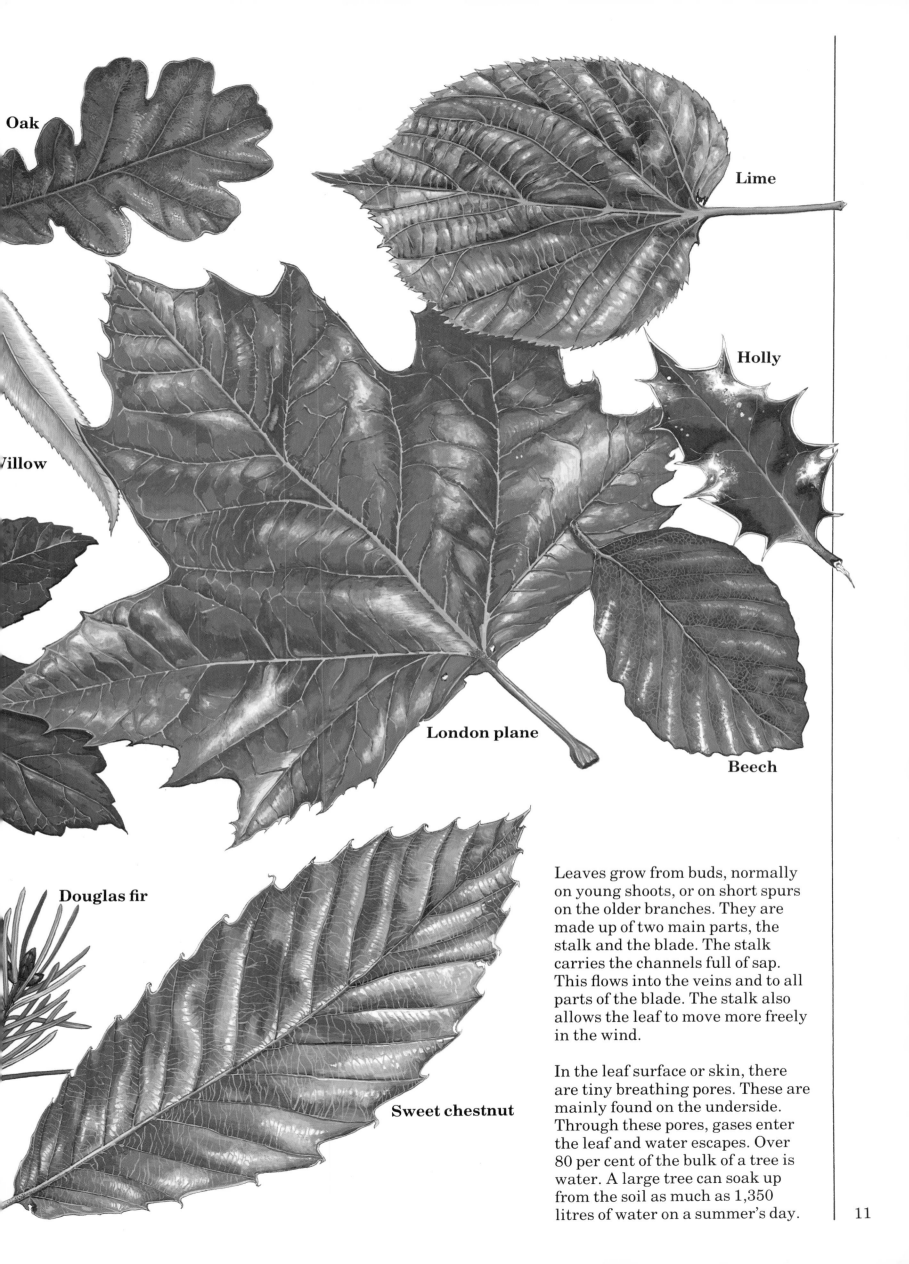

Oak

Lime

Willow

Holly

London plane

Beech

Douglas fir

Sweet chestnut

Leaves grow from buds, normally on young shoots, or on short spurs on the older branches. They are made up of two main parts, the stalk and the blade. The stalk carries the channels full of sap. This flows into the veins and to all parts of the blade. The stalk also allows the leaf to move more freely in the wind.

In the leaf surface or skin, there are tiny breathing pores. These are mainly found on the underside. Through these pores, gases enter the leaf and water escapes. Over 80 per cent of the bulk of a tree is water. A large tree can soak up from the soil as much as 1,350 litres of water on a summer's day.

11

The Flowers

When a tree is mature, it will produce flowers. From then on, it usually flowers every year. Some trees, such as the apple, cherry and hawthorn, flower at an early age. Others, such as oak, beech and pine, normally grow for many years before they are ready to flower. The flower of a tree is the first stage in forming a new tree. Flowers grow on the ends of young shoots, or on short, spur-like growths on the older branches.

A flower has several different parts. It is usually protected in bud by green scales called sepals. When these open, the petals expand. The petals are often large and colourful to attract insects. Inside the petals, is a ring of stamens like drumsticks. These are the male parts, and they contain pollen. In the centre of the flower are the styles or style. The style is the female part. It contains a tiny tube which leads to the ovary or ovaries where the ovules or eggs lie. Pollen from the stamens is carried to the style. This is usually helped by insects or by the wind. The pollen grain then grows down the tube and into the ovary. It then fertilizes the ovule.

It is only at this stage that seeds can develop. Once the ovule has been fertilized, the flower has done its job. Some tree flowers, such as those of the poplar, willow and pine, do not have sepals or petals. In these flowers, the pollen is carried by the wind. The male flowers of the pine are called catkins. In spring, the wind carries pollen from the clusters of catkins to the small red cones of the female flowers.

The flowers of most trees appear at the same time as the shoots in spring or summer. Some trees flower in autumn. A small number even flower in late winter. Those which flower in winter are usually wind-pollinated, as few insects are out and about at this time of the year.

Ants feeding on sycamore flowers

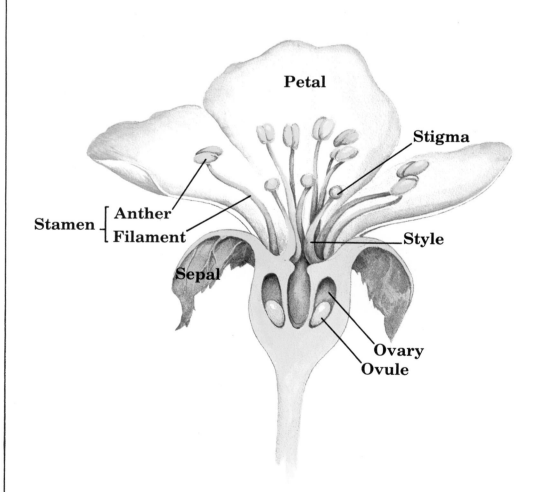

The apple flower is typical of many trees. It is easy to examine because of its size. The green sepals enclose and protect the flower when in bud. The petals are colourful and they attract insects which pollinate them. The stamens carry pollen in their anthers. The ovaries carry the ovules or eggs.

Flowers of the lime usually appear in high summer. The flowers are borne on slender stalks, and hang in bunches from the leafy shoots. They are pollinated by insects. They carry a rich supply of nectar and attract a wide range of insects, but especially all kinds of bee.

Fly feeding on pollen

Butterflies sucking nectar

Honey bee on apple blossom

More trees are pollinated by insects. The most common insect pollinators are the honey and the bumble bees. Almost as common are the butterflies with their long tongues. Many flies help pollinate some flowers, while moths are quite active, especially at night. Even ants and slugs sometimes play a part.

oplar flowers are pollinated by e wind. They usually appear in te winter, with the male and male flowers on separate trees. he individual flowers are very small. Many of them grow together in catkins, and these hang from the branches like lamb's tails. When they are ripe, as above, the grey male catkins release clouds of yellow pollen. It is blown by the wind to the female catkins. Then the male catkins shrivel and die. The female catkins become plump with fruit.

13

The Fruit

When the flower has been pollinated, fruits begin to develop. The ovary forms a protective cover or shell. Inside this shell, the fertilized ovules become seeds. In some trees, such as the apple, peach and pear, the stem immediately below the flower swells. It grows around the ovary to form a fleshy cover. It is this fleshy stem that we eat as the fruit. Conifers, such as pine and spruce, have naked seeds. These seeds do not have a fleshy cover or shell. But they do grow inside a cone. The woody scales of the cone helps to protect the delicate seeds.

Most seeds ripen in autumn. Some, such as oak and maple, will begin to grow, or germinate, as soon as they fall to the ground. Most tree seeds, however, are designed to survive the winter. They begin to germinate the following spring. Some will not germinate until the following autumn or even the year after. Seeds vary in their shape and size. Oak and chestnut seeds are large and fleshy. They are a favourite food of squirrels and mice. Other seeds, such as hawthorn, yew and cherry, have soft pulpy coats. These are much beloved by birds. Then there are trees such as alder and birch which have small flattened seeds. They blow away like confetti in the wind.

The seed contains the germ of a new tree. You can think of it as a tree kit. When conditions are right, it will germinate. Using food stored in the seed, the young tree will grow and develop.

Large fleshy fruits such as chestnuts and acorns are a favourite food of a number of small animals. These include mice, squirrels and birds of the crow family. Acorns also provide food for many insects and their larvae.

An acorn will begin to grow or germinate soon after it has fallen to the ground in early autumn. Moisture from the soil is absorbed by the seed, making it swell. Then the hard seed coat splits open.

Next, the first young root, called the radical, appears. It grows down into the soil. Later, the first young shoot, the plumule, emerges. It grows towards the light. The young root soon begins

to take in water, and the leaves of the young shoot begin to make food. The old acorn case then shrivels up. Now the seedling is on its own. If all has gone well, will grow into a healthy tree.

Plums, and other fleshy fruits such as cherries, apples and pears, are very attractive to wasps and flies. You can see them buzzing round jam-pots in the summer. These insects enjoy the sweet juice of ripe or over-ripe fruit. They will fly some distance to find it and return again and again once they have tasted it. The wasp chews the flesh of the fruit. The fly simply sucks the juice through its tongue.

Pine seeds

Ash seeds

Willows and poplars have tiny seeds hidden in white down or floss. When ripe, the small capsules containing the seeds split open. The escaping seeds are blown away in the wind.

Rowan berries

Sycamore seeds

The fruit of a tree is actually the seed together with its outer case. For example, the fruit of the oak is the acorn together with its cup. The horse chestnut fruit is made up of the conker and its prickly case.

It is important that the fruit should fall as far from the parent tree as possible. This gives it a better chance of survival. Some fruits have wings or parachutes to carry them in the wind. Ash and pine fruits have a single wing. Maple and sycamore have two wings which make them spin like propellers. Seeds of poplar and willow are fluffy. Fleshy fruits, such as berries, are eaten by mice and birds. The seeds are dropped elsewhere.

15

Deciduous Trees

Deciduous trees are the ones which shed all their leaves once a year. This usually takes place in autumn. At the same time, the tree stops growing ready for winter. Most kinds of tree growing wild in Britain and northern Europe are deciduous. They include many of our most familiar trees such as the poplar, elm, maple, beech, birch, ash and oak. In northern Europe, the winters are cold. If a deciduous tree did not shed its leaves and stop growing in autumn, then its young shoots would be killed by frost and cold winds. In tropical countries, and those with hot, dry climates, some of the trees shed their leaves in summer when the temperatures are at their highest.

In winter, deciduous trees show off their branch patterns most clearly. The patterns vary from one tree to another. Each tree, however, usually follows the pattern of its species. Oaks and beech, for example, have rounded crowns. The English elm has a taller, more stately outline. Other trees have slender or chimney-like crowns. Some have a weeping shape, like the willow.

In spring, when the soil warms up, the sap rises. The leaves of deciduous trees begin to come out of their buds. These first leaves are quickly followed by others. New leaves grow throughout the summer. In autumn, shorter days and colder nights arrive. The tree withdraws the food reserves from its leaves and stores them in the branches. This often causes the leaves to change colour to yellow, red, orange or brown. Finally, the leaves are shed before winter arrives.

The larch is one of the few deciduous trees that bears cones. It is a fast-growing, tall tree. The tips of the branches are pale yellow or reddish purple in winter. These create a warm attractive glow when the sun shines on them. The narrow leaves appear in spring. They grow singly on the new shoots, or in rosettes on spurs along the older shoots. The red female flowers and the yellow male flowers appear at the same time. Both grow on the same tree. The leaves are a beautiful emerald green. In autumn, the leaves turn a lovely golden yellow before falling to the ground. Then the cones are left in rows along the slender branchlets.

Horse chestnut buds in winter

Buds in early spring

Young leaves in spring

The horse chestnut is a deciduou tree. It is easy to follow the cycle its growth. The fat sticky buds of winter are well known. In spring they begin to swell and the sticky scales fall away. The buds on the stouter shoots produce flower heads with the new growth. In lat spring the leaves expand to catch the light. The flower heads grow larger. New leaves continue to appear through the summer. In autumn, they yellow before falling to the ground where they rot away.

Fruits in autumn

Flowers in early summer

e ash in winter shows off its ey grooved trunk and stout grey anches. Its leaves appear in ring, later than most other ciduous trees. The flowers, wever, are early. They appear in bunches on the naked branchlets. When the leaves expand, during the spring, each leaf has a central stalk. This central stalk has a row of leaflets on either side.

e durmast oak, or sessile oak, is nilar in many ways to the mmon or English oak. Its leaves, wever, are more tapered at the se. Its acorns do not have a stalk but sit directly on the shoots. It is a bold, imposing tree when mature, with its lobed leaves. It looks especially powerful against a winter sky.

The Lombardy poplar is a good example of how deciduous trees show off their branch patterns in winter. This is a fast-growing tree with a tall, straight, main stem. Its many branches do not spread outward as in most other trees. They grow upwards, at a steep angle, close to the main stem of the tree. A single tree looks very like a sentinel. A row of trees resembles a line of guardsmen on parade. In summer, the leaves are green and diamond-shaped.

Evergreen Trees

Evergreen trees do not shed all their leaves each autumn like deciduous trees. Instead, the leaves are shed gradually, and last longer than one year. At no time is the evergreen tree completely without leaves.

Evergreen trees are easier to see in winter, when deciduous trees are leafless. They appear, dark-crowned, in gardens, parks and the countryside. In many countries, evergreens are used to decorate the home, especially in winter when other trees are bare.

There are two main groups of evergreen trees. First, there are the broad-leaved evergreens, such as the holly, holm oak and strawberry tree. Then there are the evergreen conifers, such as the pine, fir and cypress. In the wild, broad-leaved evergreens are mainly found in the warmer parts of the world. There are very few kinds in Britain and northern Europe. Conifers mainly grow in the cooler parts of the world. There are many different kinds in northern Europe.

In warmer climates, the heat causes water to be lost more quickly from the leaves of trees. In colder climates, and on high mountains, the wind has the same effect. Broad-leaved evergreens in warm climates tend to have thick, leathery leaves, often coated with a thin film of wax. This helps to cut down the loss of water through the breathing pores. Some leaves are covered with hairs, which also prevents too much water being lost. Conifers in colder climates stop water-loss by rolling their leaves tightly so that they are strap-shaped, or needle-shaped. This holds in the water.

Evergreen trees usually have two main periods of growth, first in late spring and again in late summer or early autumn. For the rest of the year they grow very slowly or not at all. Deciduous trees have a main flush of growth in spring and then grow slowly but steadily throughout the summer months.

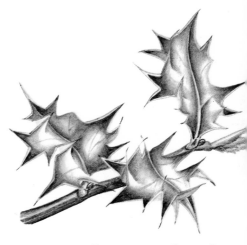

Evergreen leaves, such as those the holly, remain on the shoots f at least three years. Finally they fall to the ground, usually in summer.

The Lucombe oak is a cross between the cork oak and the Turkey oak. It is a large, heavy-crowned tree with corky bark. Its leaves are normally evergreen, but in cold winters th are sometimes shed. The male an female flowers are separate, but

The Scots pine is a common evergreen conifer in Britain and northern Europe. It is also found on mountains elsewhere. It is easily recognized by the rich orange-red bark on its upper trunk and branches. This is especially bright when the sun shines on it. Its blue-green, needle-like leaves are carried in pairs. Its seeds grow in woody cones.

18

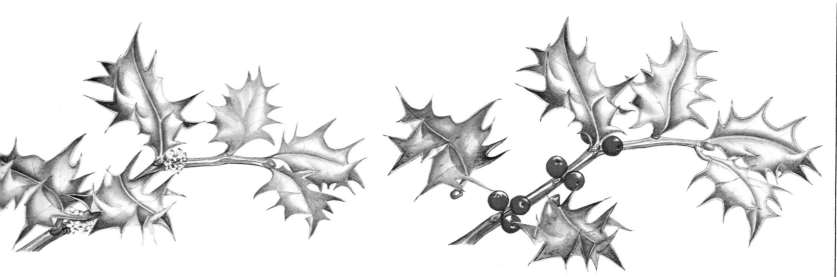

As the new shoot lengthens, its leaves expand. These leaves are soft to the touch and are not hard and spiny like the older leaves.

The young shoot emerges in late spring or early summer, when the flowers are open or have faded. Flowers are carried on shoots that grew the previous year.

The older leaves are gradually left behind. They are soon hidden in the shade of the crown. Here they often turn yellow or brown before falling.

grow on the same tree. The yellow male catkins appear in late spring or early summer. The wind carries the pollen to the tiny female flowers. Once fertilized, the female flowers produce acorns with large bristly cups. The leaves are dark, almost blackish-green.

The holly is the only broad-leaved evergreen tree native to Britain. It is also found in Europe, except in the cold areas of the north. The spine-toothed, blackish-green leaves are hard and shiny. They make an ideal setting for the bright red berries. These

cluster along the previous year's shoots throughout the winter. Male and female flowers are found on separate trees. Only the female flowers produce berries. They first have to be pollinated by the male flowers. They are usually pollinated by the wind.

Conifers

Conifers get their name because their seeds are carried in cones. Cones are usually made up of a spindle with spirals of woody scales attached to it. At first, the cone is tightly closed. The scales overlap, like the tiles or shingles on a roof. When the cone is fully ripe, the scales open wide to release the seeds. These are small and plump, like tiny nuts. They usually have a narrow wing attached. This helps the seed to be carried along by the wind.

Cones vary in size from a pea to a cannon-ball. Some cones are berry-like, as in the juniper. The yew differs again. Its seeds are carried singly in fleshy red cups.

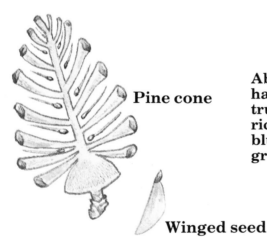

Pine cone

Winged seed

Conifers also differ from most other trees because they often have needle-like or scale-like leaves. In most conifers, the leaves are evergreen. In just a few, the leaves are deciduous, and are shed each autumn. Deciduous conifers include the dawn redwood.

Conifer leaves grow singly, in pairs or sometimes in bundles or rosettes. They are usually arranged thickly on the shoots. The new shoots start to grow in late spring.

The flowers of conifers are small and do not have petals. They normally grow together in tight heads. The male and female flowers are separate. They sometimes even grow on separate trees. When ripe, pollen from the male flowers is blown by the wind to the females.

Above: The Scots pine is a handsome evergreen. The upper trunk and main branches have a rich reddish-orange bark. The blue-green, needle-like leaves grow in pairs.

Right: The redwood is a giant evergreen, reaching heights of over a hundred metres. It has a thick, spongy, reddish-brown bark. Its leaves grow in two opposite rows.

Left: The cedar of Lebanon is easily recognized, even from a distance, by its long horizontal branches. On big tree they form layers or tiers. The large, hard cones grow on top of the branches.

Above: The Lawson cypress is a tall evergreen. It usually has a conical shape. Its small, scale-like leaves are carried in broad, flattened sprays. Its cones are smaller than a pea.

Above: The larch is one of the few deciduous conifers. It is tall and fast-growing with graceful, down-curving branches and rosettes of narrow leaves.

Left: The Douglas fir is a tall, powerful evergreen, with fragrant, needle-shaped leaves. The bark is tough and thick. The cones have three-pronged tongues growing out of them.

Above: The Norway spruce is a strong, erect-growing evergreen. It is conical in shape and its pine-tipped leaves densely crowd the branches. The cigar-shaped cones hang from the branches, falling when ripe.

Above: The yew lives to a great age. It is commonly found in churchyards. It has dark, evergreen leaves, and single seeds in red cups.

Growing Trees from Seed

Before sowing a seed, you must decide what special treatment it needs to help it germinate. Different seeds need different methods of sowing. Large, hard, but fleshy seeds, such as oak, maple and sweet chestnut, should be sown as soon as ripe. If you do not, they will dry out and will not germinate. Normally, such seeds will germinate within a few weeks of sowing. Fleshy berries, such as rowan and holly, take two years to germinate. These may be kept in sand in pots or boxes outside where the frost can soften their coats. Small seeds, such as poplar, willow, alder and birch, need a moist soil. They germinate fairly quickly when sown fresh. You can sow most other seeds in autumn to germinate in spring. Or you can store them in cool conditions until spring.

A clean pot must be used for sowing seeds. This should be scrubbed if necessary. So that excess water can escape, place a layer of pebbles in the bottom of the pot, covering the hole.

A special seed compost should be used to fill the pot to within 2 cm o the top. This compost is gritty to help drainage. Press down the compost firmly with a block or th bottom of a bottle.

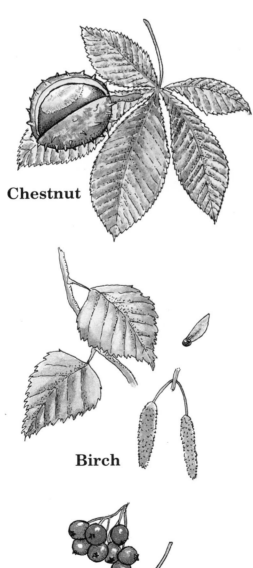

Chestnut

Birch

Rowan

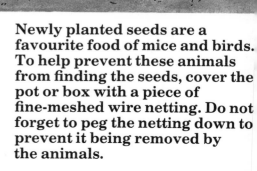

Sowing seeds out of doors can be fun. There are several ways of doing it. You can use pots, like the ones for indoor sowing. Or you can use trays or boxes. Follow the same instructions as for indoor sowing. Then, stand the pots or boxes outside, out of direct sunlight, in the shelter of a wall.

Newly planted seeds are a favourite food of mice and birds. To help prevent these animals from finding the seeds, cover the pot or box with a piece of fine-meshed wire netting. Do not forget to peg the netting down to prevent it being removed by the animals.

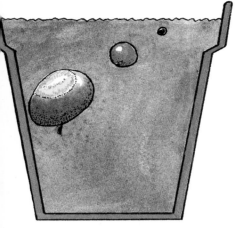

ow the seed according to its size.
simple and safe method is to sow
e seed to its own depth in the
ompost or soil. A large seed, such
s a horse chestnut, needs to be
own 2–3 cm deep. A berry, such
s a rowan, should be sown to a
epth of 1 cm. A small seed, such
s a birch or alder, needs to be
own on, or just below, the surface
f the compost. Large seeds may
e sown singly in a 10 cm pot.
mall seeds are best sown
everal to a pot.

Next, to prevent the compost from
drying out, standing the pot on a
shallow saucer or tray of water.
You can then place it by a window,
with the top covered to keep out
the light. Or you can put it in a cool
cupboard.

Another way of preventing the
compost from drying out is to
place a plastic bag over the pot.
Turn it occasionally to remove
excess moisture. It is important to
check the pot regularly to see if
the seeds have germinated.

wing seeds in the open ground
another method. This is
ecially useful for large
antities of the same seeds.
repare the ground by digging or
rking it lightly, and clearing any
eeds. Rake it carefully to remove
y large stones. Then, scoop out a
allow trench or drill with a hoe
a sharp stick. Next sow the
eds thinly along the drill, cover
em with soil and firm the soil
wn.

When the seed has germinated in
the pot, remove the polythene bag.
Put the pot in a lighty, airy place.
Once the seedlings have grown
20–30 cm high, plant them out in a
nursery bed or in the garden. Here
they can grow until they are large
enough to plant in their
permanent home. If there are
many seedlings they should be
spaced out in rows. Leave a
metre between each seedling.
Planting-out is best done in winter
when the seedlings are at rest.
Remember to sow your seeds
thinly to prevent overcrowding.
Place the seedlings out of direct
sunlight; in the shelter of a wall.

Planting a Tree

Planting a tree is a very satisfying and exciting thing to do. But if it is to grow strong and healthy, it needs special care and attention. Trees grown by nurserymen and sold through a garden centre are of several types. Some are trained so that they have a single stem with a number of small side branches. These are known as whips, and may be anything from 1–1.5 metres high. Then there are trees with a single clean stem ending in a small head of branches. Those with a clear stem of 1.5–2 metres are called standards. Those in which the clear stem is a metre or less are known as half standards. For practical reasons, standard trees have to be supported by stakes. Half standards and whips do not normally need staking, except when they are planted in very windy sites.

Nurserymen's trees also differ in the way their roots are treated. Deciduous trees are often grown in the open ground. When they are ready for sale, they are dug up in winter with the roots bare. Or they may be wrapped in plastic sacking. The roots of evergreen trees, however, must be kept in a ball of soil before they are wrapped. Many trees, however, are now grown in pots or polythene bags. They can be planted all year round.

Buying trees from a garden centre is something the whole family can enjoy. There is usually a large selection from which to choose.

Each tree has a tag with its name on it. This will help you to check out details of the tree in a catalogue or book.

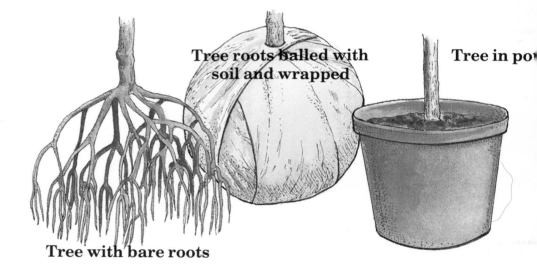

Tree roots balled with soil and wrapped

Tree in pot

Tree with bare roots

Planting trees can be fun. First choose a site in a bed or lawn. Make sure that it is not too close to the house, drive or path. Then dig a hole which is deep and wide enough to take the tree roots without having to break or bend them.

Break up the soil in the bottom of the hole to aid drainage. Next, add compost or well rotted manure, together with a handful of fertilizer such as bonemeal or super-phosphate. This will help the tree to make a good start in its new home.

Mix the fertilizer and compost with a few spadefuls of soil. If the tree has a tall stem, it will need a stout stake to prevent it being blown about. This should be firmly knocked into the hole in the ground before the tree is planted.

Professional nurserymen usually grow their trees in large numbers. Skilled craftsmen grow the trees from seed, cuttings or by special techniques called budding or grafting. New trees are being started off all the year round. The young trees or seedlings are planted out in rows with plenty of space between them. When they become taller, they are secured to canes.

Before planting, try the tree in the hole to check that it has enough room. When you are ready to plant it, carefully spread out the tree's roots so that the top roots are just below the level of the surrounding ground. This will help the tree to grow strongly.

The tree is now in position, with the roots neither too deep nor too shallow. Replace the soil over and around the roots. Take care to jog the tree up and down so that soil falls between the roots, filling up the spaces. This helps to plant the tree evenly.

If a stake is needed, the tree must be planted so that its stem is close to the stake. Once the soil is replaced, firm it down by gently trampling. Finally, fix the tree stem to the stake, using two special tree ties. These keep the stake clear of the bark.

Caring for Trees

A newly planted tree needs care if it is to grow. More young trees are lost through neglect than for any other reason. If the tree has been planted in a lawn or grass area, then a circle of soil at least a metre across must be kept clean at its base. This should be weeded, otherwise trees may be choked and starved of water and food. Sometimes a black polythene or plastic sheet is placed on the soil around the tree to prevent weeds from growing. In hot summers, the soil around newly planted trees becomes dry. They must be watered otherwise the roots will die. This is especially important the first summer after planting. In a few years, the tree will be strong enough to stand alone. The stake may then be removed and extra watering is no longer necessary.

Right: Young trees sometimes need pruning in order to train them to a good shape. Branches sprouting low on the stem, or those which rub against the stake, are cut away clean from the base. This is done with a sharp saw or secateurs.

Below: Trees need care long after they have been planted. Weeds and other plants growing close to the tree's roots use up the food and water in the soil. They should be removed as soon as they appear help the young tree grow strong and healthy.

ree ties should be checked everal times a year on young rees. This is because the tree tem grows outwards as well as pwards. Quite often the ties on a ewly planted tree are forgotten. his may result in the tree being trangled, causing the top to die or

break away in the wind. If a tie is tight, it must be loosened or removed altogether and a new tie fixed in its place. Ties which use wire, rope or string should not be employed. You can see the damage that a tight tie can do in the picture above.

Wounds on a tree must always be treated. If they are ignored, then disease and rot are likely to set in. The wound should be cleaned with a sharp knife. Any loose bits should be cut away. Then the wound must be painted with a wood sealant for protection.

Above: Professional tree surgeons are called in to deal with all major tree problems. These skilled people have a wide range of tools and equipment to help them.

KEY:
 1 Visor and ear protectors
 2 Safety harness
 3 Safety rope on saw
 4 Auger
 5 Pruning tools
 6 Secateurs
 7 Pruning saw
 8 Cavity tools
 9 Pole saw and clearing hook
10 Chain saw
11 Climbing spur and pads
12 Helmet

27

Trees and Aging

Different kinds of trees live to different ages. Many of our small trees, such as crab-apple, cherry and rowan are short-lived, lasting from 30 to 50 years. The English oak may live up to a thousand years. By far the oldest living British and European tree is the yew. There is a yew in a churchard at Fortingall, Scotland, which is said to be 1,500 years old.

Many trees reach a great size but this does not always mean that they are very old. In some younger trees, historical records may help to confirm the age, but the only sure way to tell the age of a tree is to count the annual rings. There are two methods of doing this. The easiest way is to cut the tree down with a saw. This is how many trees were dated in the past but, of course, it meant killing the tree at the same time.

Borings are now the usual method of dating. To make a boring, an auger is screwed into the tree until it reaches the centre. It is then withdrawn, bringing with it a core or cylinder of wood. By examining the core under a microscope, the annual rings can be counted.

The annual rings also contain a weather chart of the tree's life. They can tell us which years were extra dry and which were very wet. In a dry year, the rings are narrow and close together. In a wet year, the rings are broad and far apart.

Terminal bud

Lateral bud

The beech can grow very tall. Sometimes it reaches 40 metres. This tree has been 'pollarded', or pruned, years ago. As a result, many branches have grown from a short trunk. The beech is not particularly long-lived. It normally lasts for between 200 and 250 years. In the end it falls down, or slowly breaks up as disease takes a hold inside the trunk.

A tree grows in two ways, both upwards and outwards. In countries with cold winters, trees stop growing in autumn and form a terminal bud. In spring, the new shoot grows from this bud and goes on growing until autumn. You can tell the age of a shoot by counting the number of terminal bud scars.

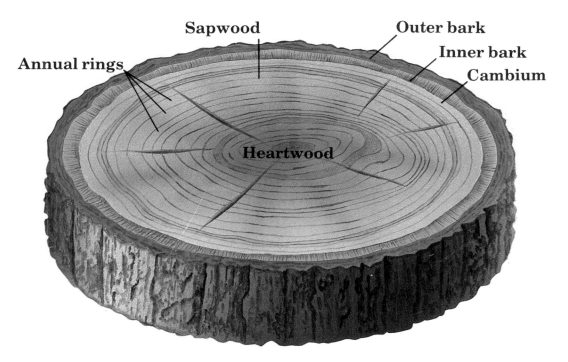

Annual rings

Sapwood

Outer bark

Inner bark

Cambium

Heartwood

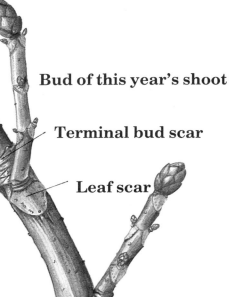

Bud of this year's shoot

Terminal bud scar

Leaf scar

Start of last year's growth

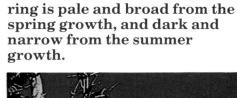

The trunk of a tree expands each year, as the cambium produces new bark and sapwood. This growth forms an annual ring. The ring is pale and broad from the spring growth, and dark and narrow from the summer growth.

The giant sequoia tree, or Wellingtonia, of California is a magnificent tree. In time it forms a tall stout trunk covered with thick spongy red bark. It lives to a great age – between 3,000 and 4,000 years. This tree is known as the General Sherman. It is the world's largest living thing. It stands 83 metres tall with a girth of 24.11 metres. This particular tree was already very large when Christ was born!

The bristlecone pine is found in the White Mountains of California. It lives to a great age – more than 4,000 years. The world's oldest living thing is a bristlecone pine of 4,600 years. The tree above is known as Alpha and is 4,300 years old. Most of the tree consists of dead wood, remarkably preserved. A strip of living bark connects the roots with a few remaining leafy branches. This pine grows very slowly.

When a Tree Dies

A tree may die from old age. Or it may die before it gets old because of injury or disease. Often one follows the other. Some trees are injured by natural causes such as lightning. This kills the top of the tree and often burns a track down through the bark to enter the ground. Severe frost or scalding sun can also kill the bark. It may cause large patches to turn black and fall away. Strong or freak winds may break branches and let disease enter into the wood. Sometimes the whole tree is blown down because the wind is so strong.

Damage may also be caused by animals, such as deer and hares, chewing or rubbing the bark. In gardens, trees are sometimes injured by dogs or cats. Trees may be killed by drought or by flooding, by pests and even vandalism. Human beings often cause tree deaths. Trees on building estates, in streets and city parks are all likely to be damaged sooner or later, and death often follows.

Very old trees sometimes become hollow before finally breaking up. When the tree finally dies, it provides a vast source of food for a whole world of living things. The stump below belongs to a deciduous tree in a forest. Parts of the trunk are lying on the ground nearby. Two large fungi are growing on the stump. Both are parasites and either one may have finally killed the tree. Mosses, ferns and lichens grow on dead bark, and several smaller fungi also find a home on it. Beetles lay their eggs in the rotting wood. Their larvae provide food for birds such as the woodpecker. Eventually all traces of the tree will vanish.

Trees can be killed by fungus diseases. These usually attack ol trees. They can also infect trees which are weakened in some wa Here, a badly damaged beech ha been attacked by a heart-rot fungus. In time the whole tree will collapse.

KEY:
1 Broad buckler fern
2 Giant grifolia
3 Violet ground beetle
4 Earthworm
5 Stag beetle larva
6 Green woodpecker
7 Verdigris fungus
8 Moss
9 Stag beetle
10 Honey fungus
11 Candle fungus
12 Roe deer
13 Centipede
14 Woodlice
15 Lichen
16 Earwig

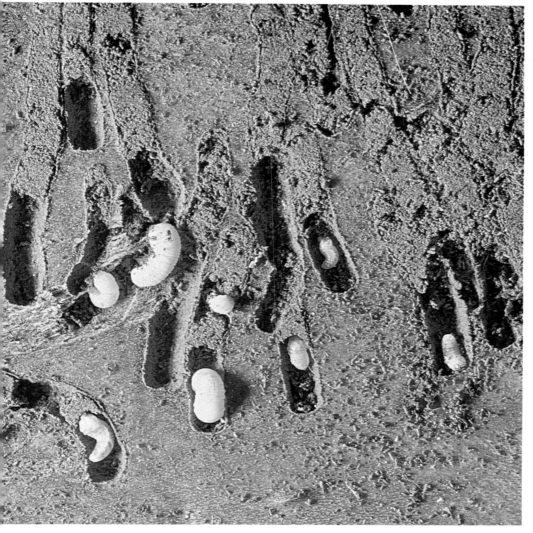

Dutch elm disease has killed millions of elms in Britain, Europe and North America. Young as well as old trees have been affected. In many parts of the countryside, their skeletons can be seen gaunt and leafless against the skyline. In time they blow down or gradually fall to pieces. Unfortunately, the disease is still spreading.

lm bark beetle larvae feed in unnels beneath the outer bark f the elm. Later they turn into dult beetles. Beetles leaving an infected tree fly off to find healthy elms. They feed on them and, in doing so, pass on the Dutch elm disease.

Making Things from Wood

Wood is one of the most important of all materials. Trees are felled and their wood used for all kinds of purposes all over the world. Our timber supplies come from natural forest, as well as from forest planted by man. Timber is divided into two main types – hardwoods and softwoods. Hardwoods come from broad-leaved trees, and softwoods come from conifers. Hardwoods have a greater range of uses than softwoods, but both are vital in their own ways.

Today, modern materials such as plastics and glass-fibre are sometimes cheaper and easier to handle than wood. However, if you look around, you will soon see that wood is used in almost every part of our daily lives. Just look round the room you are in and count the pieces of wood.

Wood is strong, light but flexible. It is very adaptable. It can be used to build a shelter, or to create a concert violin. In the hands of a craftsman, wood can be carved and polished to show off its natural grain and colour. A beautiful piece of furniture will last for hundreds of years.

At home, timber is used in the rafters, floor-boards and window-frames. It is found in the frame of the house itself, although much of this is hidden beneath brick and plaster. Wood is found in furniture and kitchen utensils. Outside, it is used to make garden sheds, fences and the handles of many tools. In sport, football and rugby posts, cricket bats, tennis rackets, skis, fishing rods, bows and arrows are all made out of wood.

Wood is also used to make many kinds of musical instruments, especially string instruments such as violins, cellos and guitars. Even pianos include a great deal of wood. Wood is still used in carriage-making, boat-building, and in country bridges. When made into pulp, wood provides most of the paper for writing, books and newspapers.

Beech is a hardwood, pinkish brown in colour, smooth and fine-grained. With oak, it is the most commonly used hardwood in Europe. It is used for tool and brush handles, kitchen utensils and furniture.

Oak is famous for its strength and long life. It has long been used in shipbuilding and to make railway carriages. It is still used for making boats, gates, doors and furniture.

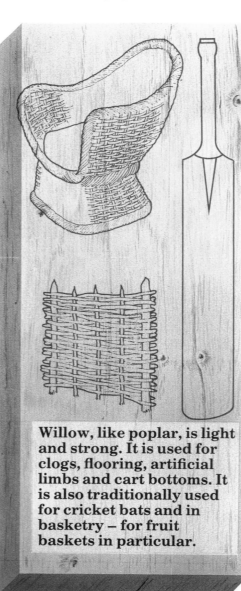

Willow, like poplar, is light and strong. It is used for clogs, flooring, artificial limbs and cart bottoms. It is also traditionally used for cricket bats and in basketry – for fruit baskets in particular.

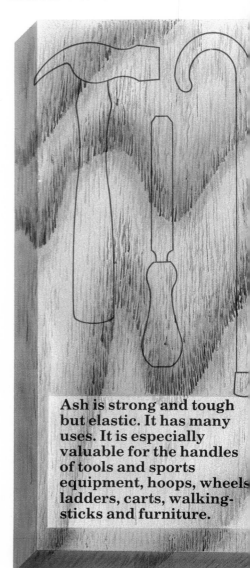

Ash is strong and tough but elastic. It has many uses. It is especially valuable for the handles of tools and sports equipment, hoops, wheels ladders, carts, walking-sticks and furniture.

ships and boats have been built from wood since ancient times. In years gone by, oak was the most commonly used timber in Britain and Europe. Most of the famous naval ships were built from oak. Here, by a small African river, a canoe is being carved from the trunk of an ebony tree. The men will take many days to make it.

Woodcarving is an ancient craft carried out all over the world. Different woods have different qualities. The craftsman gets to know how to make the best of them. Many craftsmen specialize in types of carving.

Aspen is tough but light. It is used for light structural work, as well as for veneers, boxes, crates, small household articles and matches.

Birch is hard but not long-lasting. It is used mainly for plywood, as well as for skis, veneers and for small turned objects. Its pulp is used for paper. Its twigs make brooms.

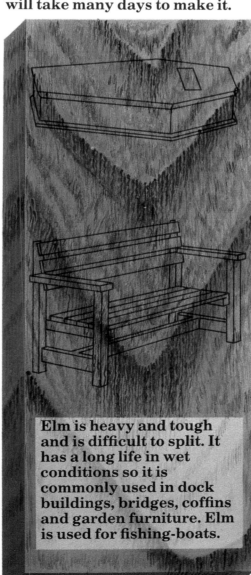

Elm is heavy and tough and is difficult to split. It has a long life in wet conditions so it is commonly used in dock buildings, bridges, coffins and garden furniture. Elm is used for fishing-boats.

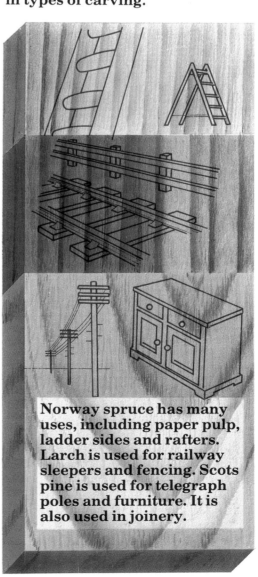

Norway spruce has many uses, including paper pulp, ladder sides and rafters. Larch is used for railway sleepers and fencing. Scots pine is used for telegraph poles and furniture. It is also used in joinery.

Trees that Feed Us

Considering how many different kinds of tree there are, fairly few of them provide us with food. Most of the ones that do give food, however, are widely grown and eaten. Most edible fruits can be found in the wild. In years gone by, they formed an important part of the diet of native peoples. This is still true in many of the countries of South America, Asia and Africa. In some countries, fruit is an essential industry.

Most important fruit trees are now grown in orchards. Here they are more easily cared for. It is also more convenient when the fruits are harvested.

Edible fruits come in many shapes and sizes, from small tough nuts to large fleshy fruits like bananas and breadfruit. Tropical fruits often seem strange and exotic. Some ripen very quickly and so do not travel well. A good number can be dried or preserved. These include the various nuts, figs, dates and those plums which are dried to make prunes.

A fruit store or market stall is an excellent place to find a selection of tree fruits. Depending on the season, there can be a wide variety of fruit for sale. This greengrocer stall is well provided.

Tree fruits are an important part of the world's food supply. In some countries, fruit-growing is an essential industry. Many countries export fruit, sending it all over the world. Most of the fruits we now eat have been specially bred. They are often larger and have greater food value than the original type. Or they may have thinner skins and fewer pips than they would have had originally.

The banana is not a real tree but a
herb. It does, however, send up a
thick, erect, trunk-like stem. This
is made of the overlapping leaf
bases. The fruits are cut in
bunches, called hands, on
drooping stalks. They are
picked green for shipping.

Dates are the fruits of the date
palm. This has been cultivated in
the Middle East for over 5,000
years. Dates grow in huge bunches
from among the leaves at the top
of the tall trunk of the date palm.
They have a high sugar and
vitamin content.

The fig is another fruit which has
been cultivated since early times.
Like the date, it is mentioned in
the Bible. It is commonly grown in
the Mediterranean region, for it
needs warmth. Figs have a high
sugar content when dry. When
eaten fresh, they are delicious and
tender. They are soft and purple in
colour when they are fresh.

Drinks are made from the fruits of
many trees. Drinks made from
citrus fruits, such as the orange,
lemon and grapefruit, are both
refreshing and good for you.

Citrus fruits are rich in vitamin C.
Some also contain sugars which
make them pleasant to eat. In this
factory, orange juice is being
bottled.

The Importance of Trees

Trees are one of the most important things in our lives. In common with other green plants, trees release oxygen. Without oxygen to breathe, we would die. Forests cover one-third of the world's land surface. They are one of our greatest resources. However, even the vast Amazon forest is threatened by our own greed and ignorance. Each day, large areas are destroyed. Forests mean more than energy and profit. They provide homes, shelter and food for countless birds, animals and insects. They also provide protection and refuge from the elements and from humans.

The life of a forest has a delicate balance which has come about after years of change and adaptation. It is easily disturbed by our interference. We must be careful not to wipe out the world's forests because once destroyed, they can never return.

We owe a great debt to trees for they have made our life on earth possible. Trees have provided us with fuel for fires to keep us warm during periods of cold, to cook our food and boil our water. Even coal comes from wood. It is a fossilized fuel made from trees which lived millions of years ago.

Trees have given us timber to build homes, villages and towns. They have also given us tools to do the job. Timber has helped us to make weapons and build defences against enemies and wild animals. It continues to be one of the most useful materials that we have.

Trees have provided paper, and enabled us to read, write and to record the history and wonders of our world. They have enabled us to travel and explore the world by land, sea and air. In many parts of the globe, trees have been used to provide clothing, fodder for cattle, and shelter from the elements. They have helped us to make music and to enjoy many sporting activities. Finally, they give pleasure. Planted beside roads and houses, trees soften the harsh effect of new building. They landscape and disguise some of the harder edges of modern architecture.

Trees planted as screens or hedg protect crops and gardens from strong or cold winds. They are particularly useful in coastal areas, open plains and on

Burning wood as fuel is one of the most widespread uses of trees. In Britain and Europe, wood is burned to heat private homes. Its main use here is in winter. The wood is burned in open-fronted grates or in stoves specially built for the purpose. In many other countries of the world, especially in isolated and wild regions, wood is used all year round. Wood fires are essential to provide heat for cooking. To these Nepalese tribesmen, a fire means life. They take fuel from the forests and carry it up into the mountains.

Trees give shade from the summe sun as well as shelter from wind and rain. They offer a refuge to domestic animals, such as the horses in this picture. Wild

illsides. Here, a row of Lombardy oplars has been planted around n apple orchard. The trees veaken the wind's power. They lso add interest to the landscape.

Planted in towns and cities, trees have a softening effect. They break up hard or straight lines and help to hide ugly buildings. Trees in parks and in city squares create green oases. They give

shelter from the noise of traffic and provide a peaceful place to rest or play. In the two pictures above you can see the difference that trees can make to a town street.

animals, for example lions in Africa, also enjoy the cool shade given by trees. Smaller animals and birds make their homes in holes in the trunk or in the

branches. The flowers of trees attract many insects which gather to feed on the nectar or pollen. The insects, in turn, pollinate the trees. Trees create a world for wildlife.

In the past, dates were one of the main foods for many people who lived in the Middle East. Trees are very important as sources of food. Most people include some fruit in their diet. In Europe the variety found in the wild is limited. In warmer countries, wild and edible tree fruits are more plentiful. The most important fruit trees are now grown in orchards. They are carefully tended so that they will produce larger and better crops. Thanks to modern transport methods, exotic fruits are now on sale in the western world all year round. Trees also provide fodder for animals.

The World of a Tree

No tree is ever alone. It gives food and shelter to a host of insects as well as birds and mammals. Some trees are richer in life than others. The English oak, for instance, attracts at least 284 different insects, the willow 266, the birch 229 and the hawthorn 149. Britain's only native broad-leaved evergreen tree, the holly, attracts a mere seven. Trees with rugged bark, such as the oak, offer greater shelter to insects.

Aphids are some of the most common and easily seen insects on trees. They suck the sap from the leaves. The larvae of leaf miners tunnel their way through the tissues of the leaf, leaving pale squiggly patterns. Watch out for oak apples and other galls. They contain the larvae of small wasps and flies. Birds and small mammals are also attracted to trees, in search of food and shelter.

The rook is a member of the crow family. Most crows build their nests in trees, usually high up in the branches. Rooks build their nests together in groups called rookeries. They lay their eggs and bring up their young in early spring. There are often as many as a hundred pairs of rooks nesting together. The nests are very big and are made of twigs and straw.

This little owl has made its nest in a hole in a tree. Several other owls nest in such places. They often stay there during the day and come to hunt after dark. They have very good hearing and vision. This, together with their silent flight, means that they can catch small mammals and insects. Some owls also eat fish, and even small reptiles. Although owls mostly hunt by night, some look for food in the daytime.

These cherry galls on the underside of an oak leaf were made by a gall wasp. In the background you can see spangle galls caused by another wasp. Galls are caused usually when insects lay their eggs in leaves, shoots or roots. The insect pierce the skin of the leaf, shoot or root. The tree reacts by producing a protective covering which is placed over the eggs. Gall wasps are very tiny, only a few millimetres long.

The woodmouse, or long-tailed field mouse, often makes its burrow under the roots of trees. It is just as much at home in the garden as in the hedgerow. It collects and hoards grain and fallen berries. The woodmouse is the most common mouse in the European countryside.

The red squirrel is one of the most charming of Europe's smaller mammals. It builds its home, called a drey, in the angle of a branch. It feeds on seeds, shoots and eggs. The grey squirrel is now more common in Britain and northern Europe. It is not a native of Britain, but was introduced into it. It adapted very quickly, driving away the red squirrel.

This eyed hawk moth caterpillar is feeding on the leaves of a willow tree. The adult caterpillar lays its eggs on the undersides of leaves and a single female can lay up to 250 eggs over four or five days. You are likely to find eyed hawk moth caterpillars in woods where poplar, willow and apple trees grow. As these caterpillars arch themselves into a shape like the Egyptian sphinx, the moths they turn into are sometimes called 'sphinx moths'.

The lesser spotted woodpecker is a summer visitor to Britain. Like other woodpeckers, it relies heavily on trees for its food. It will often search for grubs and insects in decayed wood. It pecks away the wood with its strong beak and catches the insects with its long tongue. It also builds its nest in a hole which it bores in the living wood of a tree. Woodpeckers have strong feet and hard tail feathers for balance.

Native Trees

Britain has very few native trees compared with most other countries. Before the Ice Age began, over a million years ago, Britain had a rich variety of trees. Now there are about 35. Most are widely found in Europe as well. Just a few are found nowhere else. Although they are few in number the native trees include some of the loveliest and most useful in the world. Few trees can rival the beech in spring and autumn. Even fewer can match the English oak for strength, long life and the variety of wildlife it shelters. Most of Britain's trees are deciduous. Only the holly, yew and Scots pine are not.

Above: The English oak is probably the best known and loved native tree. It reaches as much as 30 metres, and can live up to 1,000 years. It is common throughout Europe but prefers heavy soils. Few trees attract such a wealth of wildlife, especially insects. It provides one of the most important of all timbers.

Left: The alder is a very common waterside tree. It can grow as tall as 26 metres but is normally much smaller. The male catkins open in spring, hanging like yellow lambs' tails. The tiny female flower-heads turn into small, woody, cone-like fruits.

Above: The English elm is a stately tree when mature. It can reach 30 metres or more. Its distinctive shape used to be a familiar sight along hedgerows in many parts of Britain. It was a popular tree with painters and poets, and they have often sung its praises. Since the ravages of Dutch elm disease, however, it has disappeared from many areas. This is especially true in the southern half of England.

Above: The beech is one of Europe's largest trees. It reaches as much as 40 metres when mature. In Britain it is only truly native in southern England and Wales. The flowers are small, appearing with the leaves in spring. They are followed, in a good year, by small, brown, three-cornered nuts or mast.

40

Above: The birch is a tall, slender tree with silvery-white bark and graceful drooping branches. Its diamond-shaped leaves turn yellow in autumn. It is a fast-growing but short-lived tree, and has a rather shallow root system.

Above: The crack willow and the white willow are the two most common native willows by rivers, ponds and streams. Both may reach 25 metres but they are more often pollarded, or pruned, to a short trunk. Their leaves are bright green or paler and hairy.

Left: The wild cherry can reach a height of 25 m or more. It has a smooth, dark purple bark which peels away in narrow curly strips. The white flowers crowd the long branches during the spring.

Above: The ash is a fast-growing tree which reaches 35 m or more. It is a common tree in most of Britain and Europe, and prefers well-drained soils over limestone or chalk. The dark purple flower clusters appear on the grey branches before the leaves emerge. They are replaced by winged fruits known as keys.

Left: The yew is a common tree of chalk downs in the south of Britain. It is also a familiar sight in churchyards, where it reaches a great age. The oldest yew in Britain is 1,500 years old. Many old yews are hollow.

Exotic Trees

When the Romans occupied Britain, they brought with them such trees as the bay and the sweet chestnut. Ever since, trees from distant parts of the world have come to Britain. Plant explorers, sea captains and ordinary travellers have collected seeds and seedlings of trees to grow in our gardens, estates and parks. Tree enthusiasts have even planted collections of trees, known as arboreta. Many are open to the public. In Britain and northern Europe, only those trees from the cool areas of the world are hardy enough to be grown outside. The greatest number of exotic trees in the gardens and parks of Europe come from North America and Eastern Asia – seeds of new trees are still coming from China.

The Atlas cedar is a native of the Atlas mountains of North Africa. It can grow to a great size. Its tiered branches are a familiar sight in parks and large gardens. The Atlas cedar was first brought to Britain in 1840.

Below: The tulip tree is a native of eastern North America. It was introduced to Britain before 1688.

NORTH AMERICA

California ___

SOUTH AMERICA

Chile

The Wellingtonia, or giant sequoia, is the world's biggest tree. It is a native of the mountains of California, and was first introduced into Britain in 1853. It is commonly seen in parks and large estates but these are old trees as it is less often planted nowadays.

The monkey puzzle is one of the strangest-looking trees. It has spine-tipped leaves in spirals and huge and heavy green cones the size of pineapples. It is a native of the Andes of Chile and Argentina and was brought to Britain in 1795.

The Judas tree, legend has it, is the tree upon which Judas Iscariot hung himself. It is a native of the eastern Mediterranean

Above: The ginkgo is an incredible tree, related to the conifers. Trees almost identical to it lived on earth 160 million years ago. It is a native of China.

There are a great many varieties of Japanese cherry. Most were originally introduced from the gardens of Japan. Their beautiful pink or white flowers appear in spring.

EUROPE
— Mediterranean region

ASIA
China — Japan

Himalayan region —
North Africa

AFRICA

AUSTRALASIA

Australia

Above: The tree magnolia is a native of the mountain forests of the eastern Himalaya and South-west China. It is a spectacular sight in late winter when the large pink flowers appear. It was brought to Britain in 1865.

...gion and enjoys long hot ...mmers. It was first introduced ...o Britain over 300 years ago and ...oks very exotic.

Gum trees, or eucalyptus, are mostly natives of Australia. There are over 300 different kinds, most of them fast growing. The first was brought to Britain before 1800. They are now often seen in the gardens and parks of northern Europe.

Index